Just Words Unless ...

A kids' guide to creating a kinder world

BY CHERYL KLEIN-SLEBIODA

ILLUSTRATED BY LAURA KLAMBURG

ISBN: 978-1-7353023-0-0 (hard cover)
978-1-7353023-9-3 (soft cover)

Edited by: Melissa Long

Published by Warren Publishing
Charlotte, NC
www.warrenpublishing.net
Printed in the United States

ACKNOWLEDGMENTS

It truly takes a village sometimes .... This idea started as a simple, homemade birthday gift to Anthony. Anthony's parents, Charley and Melissa Trask, loved the idea of this book for him, and it has evolved into what you are holding right now. Charley and Melissa have been with me from the beginning, and Charley's early editing help and their encouragement and excitement have been priceless. My friends and coworkers, Brian Anderson and Cheryl Schultz, insisted I "had something here." Brian would not let me let it go. Without these four, I would have never pursued publishing this book. Having a friend who wrote two books, I reached out to Bob Ackerman for direction and to share my first draft, which he was immediately excited about. He ignited the confidence in me to believe in something I created. I cannot thank him and everyone enough for their contributions. Thank you to Margaret for countless times being my let-me-run-this-by-you friend. Thank you to my brothers Kenny and Jim and his wife Sue for being proud and excited for me and interested in my progress throughout the process. To my friends Lewis, Gail, Bryce, Donna, Jeff and George for always checking in on me to see where I was in the process, asking how much longer, and keeping my head in the game, as they say. My niece Becky's teaching history helped me connect with the age group intended for this book, and her help has been priceless. My nephew Jimmy was my photographer, and along with his daughter Khloe—who can always make anything enjoyable just by being there—made something I dreaded fun. And last but not least, thank you to Christine, my cousin back home who provided me with a list of bookstores that might think a hometown girl's work is worth selling. I hope you know and feel how grateful I am. I love you all.

JUST WORDS UNLESS ...

As you become you and grow toward your independence, there will be choices to make for which you will be one hundred percent responsible. Those choices will directly impact how the world perceives you.

What I have to say in this book is quite simple—nothing complex, pretty basic actually. I'd like you to think about the words in each message. **They are all just words that will remain on a page unless you apply them to your life.** Kindness is just an eight-letter word you can ignore, but if you apply it to your life, it can become something so much more. Same with love, compassion, acceptance, understanding, and more. They are all just words unless you apply them.

There is no right or wrong way to use this book. You can go page by page or open it to a random page. Sometimes, stumbling upon a message may be just what you need. This is the reason I purposely did not number the pages. Maybe the message made you think differently about someone you know. Maybe it made you be kind to someone who frustrated you, or maybe it just helped you start your day with a nice thought, and that's okay too. Think about writing a promise or a goal of how you will apply the message. Then at the end of your day, take a moment to write down how the message played a part in your day, in your life, or in the choices you made.

The creation of this book started as a birthday gift to a very special nine-year-old boy, Anthony. He is always reading, being friendly and kind, being a good teammate, and being a genuinely happy boy. He means the world to me and is blessed with amazing parents. I wanted to give him something personal and different. While thinking of what he means to me, the thoughts in this book started flowing. The idea that a simple gift to one nine-year-old boy would turn into this book you are now reading is unbelievable to me. I am proof that the smallest, loving things you do can be the very thing that will change your life. My hope is that this book finds a place in your everyday experiences.

Stay true to the person you become and be amazing!

Strive to create a life of no regrets.
The reality is, we all make choices we regret;
it is a part of life.
LOVE GENTLY, be kind, be considerate,
and always make smart choices.

Notes

Live each day so when you lie down to sleep
and run the day through your mind,
you fall asleep with a SMILE.

Notes

There will be a time when someone
will ask you for help. You might be
tired or cranky, but sometimes, we just
HELP OTHERS because it's simply
the right thing to do.

Notes

Always BE KIND
and always show compassion.

Notes

What you say and do DEFINES who
you are and who you will forever be.

Notes

Give someone a random COMPLIMENT today. You may not realize how this can change their day.

Notes

You can learn something new every day
if you listen and OBSERVE.

Notes

If you're ever confronted with a violent situation, always choose to WALK AWAY. No matter how mad you are or how right the idea of hurting someone may feel, it's *never* the right thing to do. The wrong choice here could destroy your life or someone else's.

Notes

Trust me, your parents may be frustrating to you at times, and you're NOT ALWAYS going to be happy with them, but they are teaching you and directing you toward becoming an amazing human being. One day you'll truly UNDERSTAND this.

Notes

THINK outside the box. You never know what you may solve by using your imagination.

Notes

When you are faced with a big, possibly
life-changing decision that has you stuck
in fear, think about what advice you would
give the person you love the most if they
were faced with a similar choice. You
deserve that same advice for your life.
Yes, you *are* that IMPORTANT.

Notes

It doesn't matter who you LOVE,
just love someone with all your heart.

Notes

Your ACTIONS always speak louder
than your words. Never forget this.

Notes

Always say *please* and *thank you*.
Practice using GOOD manners.

Notes

Don't let someone talk you out of what you're doing just because they don't understand it. If it works for you, go with it. You be you and DISCOVER yourself.

Notes

Be good to the earth. Make choices to PRESERVE it and save its creatures.

Notes

Use a secret, surprise note to tell
someone you LOVE them.

Notes

Stay focused so your FUTURE goals
become your reality.

Notes

Tell your coach, "THANK YOU." They
devote a lot of time to coaching kids,
and most of them don't get paid a dime.

Notes

Open your eyes to the
BEAUTY of this world.
It surrounds us in so many ways.

Notes

Take the opportunity to PLAY in the rain—
leave the umbrellas and raincoats
behind and get soaked!
It feels so good.

Notes

Boys, practice being a GENTLEMAN. Simply opening the door will always be noticed and remembered. And girls, don't let this action go by without a grateful *thank you* and a smile.

Notes

It is your parents' duty to give you a home, an education, food, clothing, and healthcare. Everything else is a GIFT they are choosing to give you.

Notes

You have no idea what you are CAPABLE of. Don't be afraid to try new things.

Notes

Winning isn't everything; it's okay to lose occasionally. Turn a loss into a learning OPPORTUNITY.

Notes

Always LEARN from your mistakes and think about what you can do differently next time.

Notes

If an elderly person wants to spend time
with you, please do. Show INTEREST
and ask questions as this might be
the best part of their day. It will feel
good watching their smile grow.

Notes

Always find a way to REWARD yourself.

Notes

HELP carry the groceries into the house without being asked.

Notes

Think of OTHERS before thinking of yourself. People notice this.

Notes

VOLUNTEER for your own personal reasons or for someone else. It doesn't matter if it's the Earth, an animal, or a human—everybody and everything wins.

Notes

Surround yourself with good people;
they will ENRICH your life.

Notes

Always clean up after yourself
and RESPECT the home your
parents work hard to provide.

Notes

Do something THOUGHTFUL that others will remember about you.

Notes

Be FORGIVING and don't hold grudges.
They equal the weight of the world.
Work things out and stay friends.

Notes

When you're wishing for something so bad and wondering why it's not happening for you, realize that sometimes you may have to just LET GO and let life happen. Reasons become clear over time, and when they do, you will say, "I understand it now."

Notes

Open your mind and EXPLORE;
never stop learning.

Notes

Don't put pressure on yourself to be perfect. Humans can't ever be perfect; it's just not possible. Chasing something that does not exist will set you up for disappointment. Strive for your BEST, not for perfection.

Notes

True HAPPINESS lies in finding your calling in life. Experience different things and see what excites you the most.

Notes

Follow YOUR DREAMS, not someone else's.

Notes

Be KIND to *all* living things—a ladybug,
an animal, a tree, or a human.
They all matter.

Notes

Call someone just to say, "I thought of you, and it made me SMILE." This will brighten their day.

Notes

Lighten up and don't be so hard
on yourself. LAUGH at yourself sometimes!
Relax and embrace your beautiful,
unique awkwardness. We're all quirky
in our own ways.

Notes

Be grateful for the SIMPLE THINGS life sends your way. Don't let them go unnoticed.

Notes

Preserve, respect, and be GENTLE to
this Earth. It's the only one we have.

Notes

You are somebody's EVERYTHING.

Notes

Always CONGRATULATE the
team that beat you. They worked
just as hard as you did.

Notes

Never, ever be ungrateful.
You have so MUCH MORE
than you truly need.

Notes

Your parents do things for you simply
because they LOVE you. Return this favor.

Notes

Listen to your SOUL;
it is your life's compass.

Notes

Be INCLUSIVE and welcome
people's differences. Differences
make life more interesting.

Notes

Slow down and take in the world
around you. Listen to the birds,
watch a butterfly, notice a rainbow.
RELAX and ENJOY the raw
beauty around us.

Notes

Share yourself—you have so much to offer. Give someone the gift of you by SPENDING TIME with them.

Notes

You may not be the best at something.
Be patient with yourself and give
yourself time to GROW and LEARN.

Notes

Don't just say, "I LOVE you." Show it!

Notes

Practice what you want to be better at. Staying focused and WORKING HARD on what you love is the only way to get better at something. Hard work always pays off. Enjoy your accomplishment!

Notes

Be UNDERSTANDING of others.
They may be going through something
you are not aware of.

Notes

STAND UP for yourself and what is RIGHT. Others will see your strength and admire it.

Notes

Don't be a bully, choose to
STICK UP for others when
they are being mistreated.

Notes

Reach out to the new kid.
They NEED a FRIEND too.

Notes

Thank you !!!

Be THANKFUL for other people's generosity. Nobody *has* to give you things; they choose to.

Notes

Be the FRIEND parents are happy
to have around their children.

Notes

Don't stop working on something
until you're PROUD of it.

Notes

Tell your teacher "THANK YOU."
They chose a very challenging career.
Showing appreciation will give them
the confirmation they need to know
all their hard work is worth it.

Notes

LEAD by example; be the
one others look up to.

Notes

Pay it forward. When someone does something NICE for you, do something NICE for someone else without being asked.

Notes

Help out and do chores. Your
parents work EXTREMELY HARD
to provide everything you have.

Notes

There are people in this world who live
every day with physical challenges—none
of which they would choose.
Put yourself in their shoes. INCLUDE
THEM and do everything you can
to make them feel accepted.

Notes

See yourself as others see you.
Give yourself the CREDIT you deserve.

Notes

Sometimes, criticism HURTS.
We've all been on the
receiving end of it. Listen to it,
absorb it, and LEARN from it.

Notes

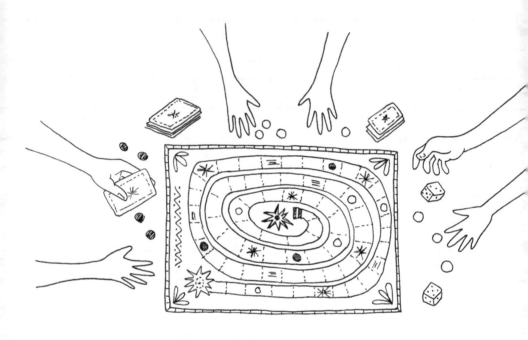

Please, don't bend the rules just
to win a game; it's just a game.
Let the one who beat you enjoy
the WIN fair and square.

Notes

If you're thinking of doing something
that doesn't feel quite right in your gut,
it's probably NOT the right thing to do.
Let it go and move on.

Notes

Mail a handwritten note instead
of texting, emailing, or FaceTiming.
It will be a WELCOME SURPRISE,
and they'll most likely keep it forever.

Notes

Give yourself some RELAXING QUIET TIME during the day. This will rest your mind and refresh your soul.

Notes

Choose a career because
you LOVE IT, not because
of the money. It will make
every day so much better.

Notes

Be brave! TRY NEW THINGS
and go on adventures. This is how
we grow, discover ourselves, and find
out where our passion lies.

Notes

Practice KINDNESS. So much comes
from this powerful word. Make being
kind natural and normal for you.

Notes

Always be a POLITE, kind,
and attentive student.

Notes

It's okay to not know the answer.
Don't get frustrated. Instead, ask
QUESTIONS, take your time and
work hard to figure it out.

Notes

You are *are* somebody's reason to SMILE.

Notes

Do the RIGHT THING even when nobody is looking. This is a true test of character.

Notes

Actually, you CAN! Don't ever let
your mind tell you that you can't.

Notes

Be a GOOD TEAMMATE and
be encouraging. Don't get angry
because someone makes a mistake.
Help them shake it off.

Notes

One KIND act can change
someone's entire day.

Notes

When you're an adult, you will find
yourself sounding like your parents.
See the BEAUTY in this.

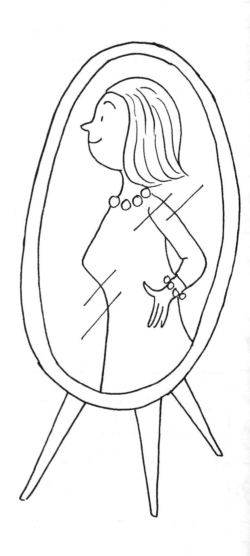

Notes

Don't give in to peer pressure just to fit in.
You'll find your place and know it when it
feels COMFORTABLE, right, and easy.

Notes

When you live a good, HONEST,
clean life, good things will start
happening for you. Please feel deserving
of these. Don't question why or
doubt them. Embrace them and
enjoy the REWARDS of your work.

Notes

Sometimes, it takes BABY STEPS to achieve something. Be patient and don't lose sight of your goal.

Notes

If there's just one thing I ask of you, it is to be KIND. Be kind to the stranger you encounter, the friend or family member you love, or the earth you stand on. This simple habit will reward you immensely and could change the world.

Notes

There's one more important thing you should understand: life is about choices. We are all responsible for where we are in life simply by the choices we make every day. Something as simple as choosing to eat a food you love even though it upsets your stomach to more complex choices that truly form your future. Making choices starts from the moment we wake up and think about the day ahead. **Please choose to stay in school and get a good education.** It's not the world's fault or anyone else's fault that you quit school and later you realize you can't get into college without a high school diploma; quitting was your choice. The choice to confront violence and not walk away from it was your choice, and now you have a criminal record and nobody will hire you. The choice to stay in that bad friendship or relationship that emotionally beats you down every day is your choice; walk away and create a safer, more loving life. Even choosing what you eat and how you treat your body makes a difference; be healthy and create the amazing you. Learn to develop the ability to redirect yourself when necessary. Life throws challenges at us and having this skill is extremely valuable. Your choices every single day are what forms your future. Be smart about life, take responsibility, and love yourself first.

Finally,

Smile so big, your eyes smile!

Be a good friend today!

Think—always think.

Always use your manners.

Be a good student.

Be understanding.

Be the best version of you.

Show compassion and kindness.

You are beautiful just the way you are.

Keep reading!

You are so incredibly loved.

Keep your promises.

Imagine, believe, and achieve.

Be resilient.

Look for rainbows after it rains.

Make a positive difference today

and live a healthy, clean life.

I SINCERELY HOPE YOU ENJOYED MY BOOK.

Everything I have to say is grounded in kindness and love. These two words encompass everything this world needs and everything our lives need. I hope what I had to say makes you think and helps you make changes within yourself to be the best you and be at peace with the person you allowed yourself to become.

I ask that you be patient with yourself and slow down when things get crazy. **Think first, then react and understand that life is hard— and that's a good thing.** Life tests us, teaches us, and helps us grow. If you want better, create better. If you want love, be more loving. If you want change, start the process. And when you feel the difference, your whole world will change—I promise you!

Follow this simple yet extremely powerful concept: be kind and loving to everything.

CPSIA information can be obtained
at www.ICGtesting.com
Printed in the USA
BVHW081629230920
589455BV00010B/468